PICTURE LIBRARY

KANGAROOS
AND OTHER
MARSUPIALS

KANGAROOS
AND OTHER
MARSUPIALS

Norman Barrett

Franklin Watts

New York London Sydney Toronto

Library of Congress Cataloging-in-Publication Data

Barrett, Norman S.
    Kangaroos and other marsupials/Norman Barrett.
        p. cm. — (Picture library)
    Includes Index
    Summary: Examines a wide variety of marsupials, such as kangaroos,
    opossums, and wombats, and describes their physical
    characteristics, habits, natural environment, and evolution.
    ISBN 0-531-14113-6
    1. Marsupialia — Juvenile literature. [1. Marsupials.]
    I. Title. II. Series.
    QL737.M3B37 1990
    599.2—dc20   90-42383
                                                       CIP
                                                        AC

Designed by
Barrett and Weintroub

Research by
Deborah Spring

Picture Research by
Ruth Sonntag

Photographs by
Survival Anglia
Australian Tourist Commission
Australian Overseas Information Service, London
Queensland Tourist and Travel Corporation
South Australian Government
Peer Productions
Government of Western Australia
Australian Museum, Sydney
Victoria Tourist Commission
N.S. Barrett Collection

Illustration by
Rhoda and Robert Burns

Technical Consultant
Michael Chinery

© 1991 Franklin Watts

Franklin Watts Inc
387 Park Avenue South
New York, NY 10016

Contents

Introduction

Marsupials are a group of mammals that range from tiny shrewlike animals to large kangaroos. The young of marsupials are very small and poorly developed at birth. They continue their growth in a pouch on their mother's body.

Most species (kinds) of marsupial are found in Australia and nearby islands. These include kangaroos, koalas and bandicoots. Some marsupials live in the Americas. These include the opossums.

△ A female kangaroo with its baby, or joey, in its pouch. The joey does not leave its mother's pouch for about six months after it is born.

Marsupials include both meat-eaters and plant-eaters. Kangaroos, wallabies and wombats eat mainly grasses. The koala feeds only on the leaves of eucalyptus trees.

Possums, not to be confused with opossums, nest in trees and eat fruits, flowers and insects. They belong to a group known as phalangers. Meat-eating marsupials include the Tasmanian devil and marsupial mice.

△ A ringtail possum of Australia. Possums are tree-dwelling marsupials that feed at night.

7

Looking at marsupials

Meat-eating marsupial:
Tasmanian tiger cat

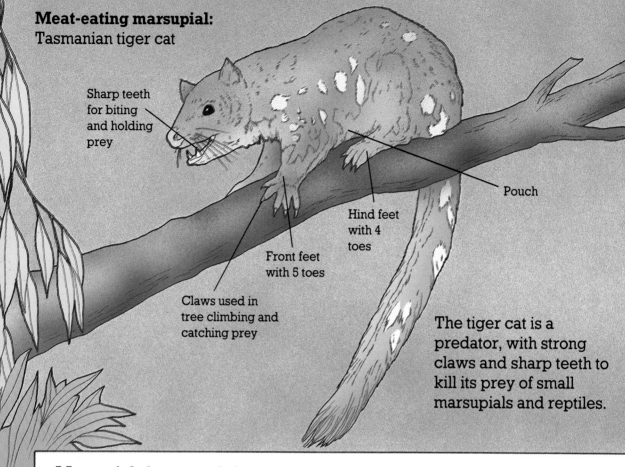

Sharp teeth for biting and holding prey

Pouch

Hind feet with 4 toes

Front feet with 5 toes

Claws used in tree climbing and catching prey

The tiger cat is a predator, with strong claws and sharp teeth to kill its prey of small marsupials and reptiles.

Marsupial shapes and sizes (body lengths)

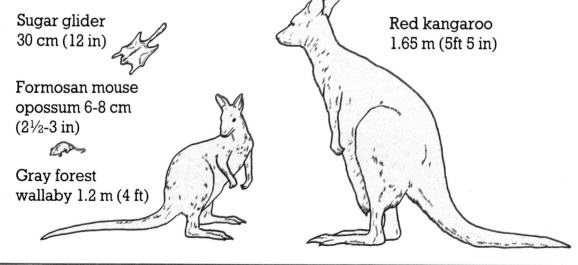

Sugar glider
30 cm (12 in)

Formosan mouse opossum 6-8 cm (2½-3 in)

Gray forest wallaby 1.2 m (4 ft)

Red kangaroo
1.65 m (5ft 5 in)

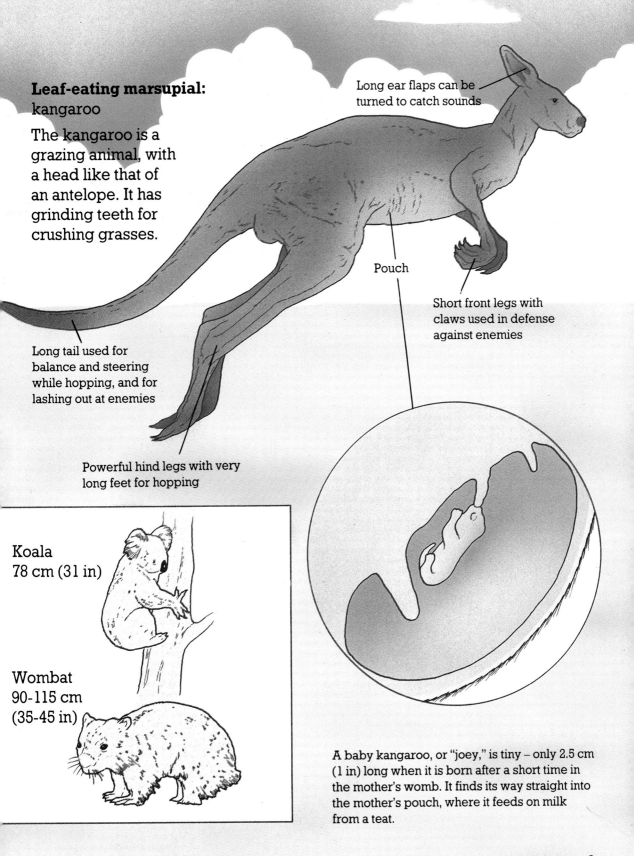

Leaf-eating marsupial:
kangaroo

The kangaroo is a grazing animal, with a head like that of an antelope. It has grinding teeth for crushing grasses.

Long ear flaps can be turned to catch sounds

Pouch

Short front legs with claws used in defense against enemies

Long tail used for balance and steering while hopping, and for lashing out at enemies

Powerful hind legs with very long feet for hopping

Koala
78 cm (31 in)

Wombat
90-115 cm
(35-45 in)

A baby kangaroo, or "joey," is tiny – only 2.5 cm (1 in) long when it is born after a short time in the mother's womb. It finds its way straight into the mother's pouch, where it feeds on milk from a teat.

9

Kangaroos and wallabies

Kangaroos, wallabies and wallaroos belong to the same family. The rat kangaroos, which include potoroos and bettongs, belong to a separate family. They are smaller than the others and less well adapted for jumping.

Most kinds of kangaroos are found only in Australia. Some species of rat and tree kangaroos also live in New Guinea and on nearby islands.

△ A parma wallaby with joey. Wallaby is the common name given to several kinds of medium-size kangaroos.

▷ A family group of red kangaroos. The name "red" can be misleading, because only those that live in western parts of Australia are red. Others may be a grayish-blue.

◁Kangaroos bound speedily across the ground by hopping on their hind legs. They usually live in small groups, and graze in the early evening. Kangaroos are found in most parts of Australia – in woodland and grasslands, on the plains and on dry, rocky hills, and even in the deserts.

△ Western gray kangaroos drinking at a watering hole. Again, the name is confusing, as both western and eastern gray kangaroos often look more red than gray.

◁ Male kangaroos sometimes fight over females. They stand on their hind legs, lock their forearms and try to push each other back onto the ground.

Kangaroos breed all year round. A single joey is born a month after mating. It is only about 2.5 cm (1 in) long, but its front legs are strong enough for it to crawl up its mother's belly and into her pouch.

The tiny joey attaches itself to one of its mother's four teats and feeds on her milk. The joey is able to leave the pouch after six months. It can continue to feed on its mother's milk even if a new joey is occupying the pouch.

▽ A two-week-old joey feeding in its mother's pouch. It is no bigger than the elongated teat next to it, which is still used to feed a big joey. The mother kangaroo produces different kinds of milk in each teat to feed the baby and older joey.

◁ A pademelon, or scrub wallaby.

▽ One of the several species of tree kangaroos. This one has the face of a bear! Tree kangaroos climb by gripping with their forelimbs and moving their hind legs separately, something other kangaroos cannot do except when swimming.

▷The quokka is a small wallaby, now known by the name given to it by the Aborigines, the original people of Australia.

▽The burrowing bettong, or boodie, one of the many kinds of rat kangaroo. It is the only kangaroo that regularly lives in burrows. It eats plants, seeds, fruit and termites.

Possums and opossums

Possums and opossums are not closely related, but are often confused because of their names.

Opossums live in the Americas, from Ontario in Canada down to South America. The common opossum is the only species found in the United States. Opossums are born in litters of 5 to 20.

Possums live in trees in Australia and nearby islands. There are several species, some like squirrels and others like monkeys.

△ A woolly opossum of South America carrying a young opossum on its back. Opossums eat almost any kind of meat or plant food.

▷ The ringtail possum enjoys a meal while perched on a branch. Like many other species of possum, it is nocturnal and uses its long tail to grasp branches.

Bandicoots and bilbies

◁ The common brushtail possum is a fox-sized animal found nearly all over Australia. Except when breeding, it lives alone in its own "den tree," but it often roams over the ground at night. Brushtails often nest on the roofs of houses. They are valued for their fur.

▽ The greater bilby, also known as the rabbit-eared bandicoot.

Bandicoots are ratlike marsupials with a pointed snout and sharp teeth. Most kinds of bandicoots live in forests, but one species, the bilby, lives in the desert.

At night, bandicoots forage for food. They dig up insects, spiders, worms and other small animals. The female bandicoot has a backward opening pouch, so that it does not get filled with earth when she is digging.

Meat-eating marsupials

A number of marsupials are meat-eaters, or carnivores. Most of them belong to a family called dasyurids. There are other marsupials that eat meat, such as the opossums, but the dasyurids have special claws for killing small animals and teeth for eating flesh.

Most of the dasyurids themselves are small, no bigger than mice. Among the largest are the Tasmanian devil and the quolls. The numbat is another carnivore.

△ The Tasmanian devil has powerful jaws and teeth for eating small mammals, lizards and birds. It is mainly a scavenger, feeding on dead animals. But it also eats living prey, such as poultry or lambs.

▷ The eastern quoll, or tiger cat, also feeds on small animals.

▽ The numbat, or marsupial anteater. This carnivore does not belong to the dasyurid family, and its teeth are not used for chewing. It spends most of its time digging for termites (not ants).

Koalas and wombats

Koalas and wombats are closely related, but lead very different lives. Koalas live only in trees. The wombat lives on the ground, in burrows.

In the wild, both animals are nocturnal and usually live alone, except for a mother with her young.

The koala is sometimes called the koala bear, and it does look like a live teddy bear. But it is not related to the bear family.

▷ The koala spends most of its time in trees, coming down only to move to a new tree. Koalas sleep during the day, wedged high up in the fork of a tree.

▽ Koalas feeding on their only food – eucalyptus leaves.

◁A female koala carries her youngster up a tree. A baby koala stays in its mother's pouch for seven months and is carried on her back for another five.

Wombats have powerful legs, and long, strong claws for digging their burrows. In Australia they are often called badgers. They feed on grasses and roots of trees and shrubs.

The female wombat usually has just one baby. It feeds in her pouch for six months, and then remains by her side for nearly a year, learning how to burrow and where to find food.

◁ The wombat is a chunky animal, like a small bear, with soft fur and no tail.

The story of marsupials

The first marsupials

Scientists believe that about 100 million years ago marsupials developed on a large continent that later split up to become America, Antarctica and Australia.

Many of the American marsupials became extinct (died out) because of competition for food and space with other mammals, especially rodents and hooved animals, which moved down from the north before South America was completely cut off. When, just a few million years ago, North and South America became rejoined by land, jaguars

△ A reconstruction of the marsupial lion, thought to have become extinct some 30,000 years ago. Although lionlike, it was related to the koalas and wombats of today and was probably a tree-dweller.

and other large carnivorous animals moved south. As a result, the larger carnivorous marsupials also died out. But some marsupials survived, the ancestors of today's opossums. The common opossum even spread north and colonized North America.

Australian marsupials did not face the same competition from other mammals. They flourished, and there are now nearly 200

△ The Tasmanian tiger, a wolflike marsupial now thought to have been hunted to extinction. No confirmed sightings have been made since the last one was captured in 1933.

different species of marsupials living in Australia, New Guinea and nearby islands.

Marsupials of yesterday
From fossil remains, scientists have reconstructed some of the marsupials of the past. Millions of years ago there was a jaguar-sized sabre-toothed tiger in South America, similar to the tigers on other continents. A giant kangaroo 3 m (10 ft) tall, once lived in Australia. The marsupial lion, one of the strangest creatures, probably died out only 30,000 years ago. The bulky, bearlike "diprotodon" is thought to have survived until 20,000 years ago.

The largest of the recent marsupial carnivores thought to have died out was the Tasmanian tiger, or wolf. A wolflike animal, it was once found throughout Australia and New Guinea. But this century it has been known only in Tasmania, the Australian island southeast of the mainland.

Marsupials in danger
Many Australian marsupials are in danger of extinction, as people destroy their habitats for farmland or to build cities. Their lives are also threatened by animals introduced by humans, such as dogs and foxes. Rabbits compete for food and space. Among the marsupials in great danger of extinction are a species of hairy-nosed wombat and the numbat.

Protection
The most endangered marsupials are now protected by law, as are many other species, such as koalas and some kangaroos, once hunted for their fur or skins.

Areas have been set aside as wildlife parks and animal sanctuaries. The Australian government and those of the individual states are taking steps to prevent further destruction of habitats. It is hoped that their actions are not too late.

Facts and records

△ The Tasmanian devil is a frightening sight when it opens its mouth. It can crush the skull of a sheep in its powerful jaws.

What a devil!

When the Tasmanian devil opens its mouth, showing its powerful teeth and letting out its bloodcurdling cry, it is a fearful sight. The first European settlers in Australia thought it looked "the very devil" of an animal, and that's how it got its name. But these black-furred marsupials do not attack humans.

Rapid breeders

Bandicoots are the fastest breeders of all mammals. In some species, the gestation period – the time between mating and having their young – is only $12\frac{1}{2}$ days. A newborn baby may be only 13 mm ($\frac{1}{2}$ in) long.

Playing possum

The phrase to "play possum" means to pretend to be dead. It comes from the habit of opossums, when in danger, of lying still and appearing to be dead.

"Rat nest" island

When Dutch explorers first came upon Rottnest Island, off the western Australian coast, near Perth, they thought it was overrun by large rats. So they named the island Rottnest, meaning "rat nest." But they were not rats – they were tiny wallabies now known as quokkas!

△ A wildlife officer feeds a quokka on Rottnest Island.

Glossary

Carnivore
A carnivorous, or meat-eating, animal.

Extinct
A species is extinct when there are no longer any living.

Fossil
Ancient bones or the impression of the remains of an animal preserved in rock.

Habitat
The type of area where an animal lives, such as rainforest or desert.

Joey
A baby kangaroo.

Litter
All the babies born to a mother at one time.

Mammal
An animal with body hair and mammary glands, or breasts, with which the mother suckles her young.

Marsupials
Mammals in which the females give birth to their young before they are fully developed. Development is completed in a pouch outside the body.

Nocturnal
Active at night.

Prey
An animal killed by another animal for food.

Scavenger
An animal that feeds on the flesh of dead animals.

Species
A particular kind of animal or plant. Animals of the same species breed young of that species.

Suckle
Female mammals suckle their young, nursing them on their own milk.

Teats
The tops of a nursing mother's milk glands, through which the young suck milk.

Wallaby
The common name used for some medium-sized species of kangaroo.

Womb
The place inside a mother's body in which the young develop before they are born.

Index